AF684104

GOD'S WISDOM FOR HANDLING MONEY

The Best In Wholesome Reading
CHOICE BOOKS Dept. 243
11923 Lee Highway
Fairfax, VA 22030
We Welcome Your Response

All Scripture taken from THE HOLY BIBLE
King James Version

GOD'S WISDOM FOR HANDLING MONEY

Copyright © 1994
Robert A. Reynhout

Published By:
PR Ministries
601 S.W. Adams
Peoria, IL 61602
Ph. (309) 676-6416
FAX (309) 676-4334

ISBN: 0-9646412-0-8

God's Wisdom For Handling Money

God's Wisdom For Handling Money is a topical guide from Scripture to help you experience freedom in handling finances. God's Word is God breathed and is useful for instruction in decision making. This reference collection of verses will help identify money issues important to you.

As you meditate on God's Word for answers to your financial questions, you will discover that *God's Wisdom* is more profitable than silver and yields better returns than gold. *God's Wisdom* is more precious than rubies, and nothing you desire can compare to it.

CONTENTS

What Does The Bible Says About...

Jesus

For God so loved the world, that he gave his only begotten Son, that whosoever believeth in him should not perish, but have everlasting life. For God sent not his Son into the world to condemn the world; but that the world through him might be saved.

John 3:16,17

That if thou shalt confess with thy mouth the Lord Jesus, and shalt believe in thine heart that God hath raised him from the dead, thou shalt be saved.

Romans 10:9

But God commendeth his love toward us, in that, while we were yet sinners, Christ died for us.

Romans 5:8

Therefore being justified by faith, we have peace with God through our Lord Jesus Christ:

Romans 5:1

If we confess our sins, he is faithful and just to forgive us our sins, and to cleanse us from all unrighteousness.

I John 1:9

For what the law could not do, in that it was weak through the flesh, God sending his own Son in the likeness of sinful flesh, and for sin, condemned sin in the flesh: That the righteousness of the law might be fulfilled in us, who walk not after the flesh, but after the Spirit.

Romans 8:3-4

That which we have seen and heard declare we unto you, that ye also may have fellowship with us: and truly our fellowship is with the Father, and with his Son Jesus Christ.

I John 1:3

For ye are all the children of God by faith in Christ Jesus.

Galatians 3:26

For he hath made him to be sin for us, who knew no sin; that we might be made the righteousness of God in him.

II Corinthians 5:21

All things were made by him; and without him was not any thing made that was made.

In him was life; and the life was the light of men.

John 1:3-4

And we know that the Son of God is come, and hath given us an understanding, that we may know him that is true, and we are in him that is true, even in his Son Jesus Christ. This is the true God, and eternal life.

I John 5:20

When Christ, who is our life, shall appear, then shall ye also appear with him in glory.

Colossians 3:4

How God anointed Jesus of Nazareth with the Holy Ghost and with power: who went about doing good, and healing all that were oppressed of the devil; for God was with him.

Acts 10:38

Who, being in the form of God, thought it not robbery to be equal with God:

But made himself of no reputation, and took upon him the form of a servant, and was made in the likeness of men:

And being found in fashion as a man, he humbled himself, and became obedient unto death, even the death of the cross.

Wherefore God also hath highly exalted him, and given him a name which is above every name:

That at the name of Jesus every knee should bow, of things in heaven, and things in earth, and things under the earth;

And that every tongue should confess that Jesus Christ is Lord, to the glory of God the Father.

Philippians 2:6-11

He is despised and rejected of men; a man of sorrows, and acquainted with grief: and we hid as it were our faces from him; he was despised, and we esteemed him not.

Surely he hath borne our griefs, and carried our sorrows: yet we did esteem him stricken, smitten of God, and afflicted.

But he was wounded for our transgressions, he was bruised for our iniquities: the chastisement of our peace was upon him; and with his stripes we are healed.

All we like sheep have gone astray; we have turned every one to his own way; and the LORD hath laid on him the iniquity of us all.

He was oppressed, and he was afflicted, yet he opened not his mouth: he is brought as a lamb to the slaughter, and as a sheep before her shearers is dumb, so he openeth not his mouth.

 Isaiah 53:3-7

God's Word

All scripture is given by inspiration of God, and is profitable for doctrine, for reproof, for correction, for instruction in righteousness:

II Timothy 3:16

Every word of God is pure: he is a shield unto them that put their trust in him.

Proverbs 30:5

The law of the LORD is perfect, converting the soul: the testimony of the LORD is sure, making wise the simple.

Psalm 19:7

And thine ears shall hear a word behind thee, saying, This is the way, walk ye in it, when ye turn to the right hand, and when ye turn to the left.

Isaiah 30:21

This book of the law shall not depart out of thy mouth; but thou shalt meditate therein day and night, that thou mayest observe to do according to all that is written therein: for then thou shalt make thy way prosperous, and then thou shalt have good success.

Joshua 1:8

Happy is the man that findeth wisdom, and the man that getteth understanding.

For the merchandise of it is better than the merchandise of silver, and the gain thereof than fine gold.

She is more precious than rubies: and all the things thou canst desire are not to be compared unto her.

Length of days is in her right hand; and in her left hand riches and honour.

Proverbs 3:13-16

Forever, O LORD, thy word is settled in heaven.

Psalm 119:89

Thy word is a lamp unto my feet, and a light unto my path.

Psalm 119:105

We have also a more sure word of prophecy; whereunto ye do well that ye take heed, as unto a light that shineth in a dark place, until the day dawn, and the day star arise in your hearts:

Knowing this first, that no prophecy of the scripture is of any private interpretation.

For the prophecy came not in old time by the will of man: but holy men of God spake as they were moved by the Holy Ghost.

II Peter 2:19-21

What God Says About...

The Love of Money

No servant can serve two masters: for either he will hate the one, and love the other; or else he will hold to the one, and despise the other. Ye cannot serve God and mammon.

And the Pharisees also, who were covetous, heard all these things: and they derided him.

Luke 16:13-14

But they that will be rich fall into temptation and a snare, and into many foolish and hurtful lusts, which drown men in destruction and perdition.

For the love of money is the root of all evil: which while some coveted after, they have erred from the faith, and pierced themselves through with many sorrows.

I Timothy 6:9-10

Then Jesus beholding him loved him, and said unto him, One thing thou lackest: go thy way, sell whatsoever thou hast, and give to the poor, and thou shalt have treasure in heaven: and come, take up the cross, and follow me.

And he was sad at that saying, and went away grieved: for he had great possessions.

And Jesus looked round about, and saith unto his disciples, How hardly shall they that have riches enter into the kingdom of God!

And the disciples were astonished at his words. But Jesus answereth again, and saith unto them, Children, how hard is it for them that trust in riches to enter into the kingdom of God!

It is easier for a camel to go through the eye of a needle, than for a rich man to enter into the kingdom of God.

And they were astonished out of measure, saying among themselves, Who then can be saved?

Mark 10:21-26

For what is a man advantaged, if he gain the whole world, and lose himself, or be cast away?

Luke 9:25

He that loveth silver shall not be satisfied with silver; nor he that loveth abundance with increase: this is also vanity.

Ecclesiastes 5:10

No man can serve two masters: for either he will hate the one, and love the other; or else he will hold to the one, and despise the other. Ye cannot serve God and mammon.

Matthew 6:24

Wealth

Labour not to be rich: cease from thine own wisdom.

Wilt thou set thine eyes upon that which is not? for riches certainly make themselves wings; they fly away as an eagle toward heaven.

Proverbs 23:4-5

A good name is rather to be chosen than great riches, and loving favour rather than silver and gold.

Proverbs 22:1

In the house of the righteous is much treasure: but in the revenues of the wicked is trouble.

Proverbs 15:6

The blessing of the LORD, it maketh rich, and he addeth no sorrow with it.

Proverbs 10:22

But thou shalt remember the LORD thy God: for it is he that giveth thee power to get wealth, that he may establish his covenant which he sware unto thy fathers, as it is this day.

Deuteronomy 8:18

Wealth and riches shall be in his house: and his righteousness endureth for ever.

Psalm 112:3

And I will shake all nations, and the desire of all nations shall come: and I will fill this house with glory, saith the LORD of hosts.

The silver is mine, and the gold is mine, saith the LORD of hosts.

Haggai 2:7-8

Trust not in oppression, and become not vain in robbery: if riches increase, set not your heart upon them.

Psalm 62:10

He that trusteth in his riches shall fall: but the righteous shall flourish as a branch.

Proverbs 11:28

But they that will be rich fall into temptation and a snare, and into many foolish and hurtful lusts, which drown men in destruction and perdition.

I Timothy 6:9

Lay not up for yourselves treasures upon earth, where moth and rust doth corrupt, and where thieves break through and steal:

But lay up for yourselves treasures in heaven, where neither moth nor rust doth corrupt, and where thieves do not break through nor steal:

Matthew 6:19-20

Forasmuch as ye know that ye were not redeemed with corruptible things, as silver and gold, from your vain conversation received by tradition from your fathers;

I Peter 1:18

Surely every man walketh in a vain shew: surely they are disquieted in vain: he heapeth up riches, and knoweth not who shall gather them.

Psalm 39:6

But the rich, in that he is made low: because as the flower of the grass he shall pass away.

For the sun is no sooner risen with a burning heat, but it withereth the grass, and the flower thereof falleth, and the grace of the fashion of it perisheth: so also shall the rich man fade away in his ways.

James 1:10-11

Go to now, ye rich men, weep and howl for your miseries that shall come upon you.

Your riches are corrupted, and your garments are motheaten.

Your gold and silver is cankered; and the rust of them shall be a witness against you, and shall eat your flesh as it were fire. Ye have heaped treasure together for the last days.

James 5:1-3

They that trust in their wealth, and boast themselves in the multitude of their riches;

None of them can by any means redeem his brother, nor give to God a ransom for him:

Psalm 49:6-7

Be not thou afraid when one is made rich, when the glory of his house is increased;

For when he dieth he shall carry nothing away: his glory shall not descend after him.

Psalm 49:16-17

For it is easier for a camel to go through a needle's eye, than for a rich man to enter into the kingdom of God.

Luke 18:25

Charge them that are rich in this world, that they be not highminded, nor trust in uncertain riches, but in the living God, who giveth us richly all things to enjoy;

1 Timothy 6:17

There is that maketh himself rich, yet hath nothing: there is that maketh himself poor, yet hath great riches.

The ransom of a man's life are his riches: but the poor heareth not rebuke.

Proverbs 13:7-8

The rich man is wise in his own conceit; but the poor that hath understanding searcheth him out.

A faithful man shall abound with blessings: but he that maketh haste to be rich shall not be innocent.

He that hasteth to be rich hath an evil eye, and considereth not that poverty shall come upon him.

Proverbs 28:11,20,22

Riches profit not in the day of wrath: but righteousness delivereth from death.

Proverbs 11:4

Inheritance

A good man leaveth an inheritance to his children's children: and the wealth of the sinner is laid up for the just.

Proverbs 13:22

House and riches are the inheritance of fathers: and a prudent wife is from the LORD.

Proverbs 19:14

If a man beget an hundred children, and live many years, so that the days of his years be many, and his soul be not filled with good, and also that he have no burial; I say, that an untimely birth is better than he.

Ecclesiastes 6:3

An inheritance may be gotten hastily at the beginning; but the end thereof shall not be blessed.

Proverbs 20:21

Behold, the third time I am ready to come to you; and I will not be burdensome to you: for I seek not yours, but you: for the children ought not to lay up for the parents, but the parents for the children.

II Corinthians 12:14

Lest there be any fornicator, or profane person, as Esau, who for one morsel of meat sold his birthright.

For ye know how that afterward, when he would have inherited the blessing, he was rejected: for he found no place of repentance, though he sought it carefully with tears.

Hebrews 12:16-17

Yea, I hated all my labour which I had taken under the sun: because I should leave it unto the man that shall be after me.

Ecclesiastes 2:18

And he said unto me, It is done. I am Alpha and Omega, the beginning and the end. I will give unto him that is athirst of the fountain of the water of life freely.

He that overcometh shall inherit all things; I will be His God, and he shall be my son.

Revelation 21:6-7

I lead in the way of righteousness, in the midst of the paths of judgment:

That I may cause those that love me to inherit substance; and I will fill their treasures.

Proverbs 8:20-21

For there is a man whose labour is in wisdom, and in knowledge, and in equity; yet to a man that hath not laboured therein shall he leave it for his portion. This also is vanity and a great evil.

Ecclesiastes 2:21

Budgeting

A man's heart deviseth his way: but the LORD directeth his steps.

Proverbs 16:9

Be thou diligent to know the state of thy flocks, and look well to thy herds.

For riches are not for ever: and doth the crown endure to every generation?

Proverbs 27:23-24

Through wisdom is an house builded; and by understanding it is established:

Proverbs 24:3

The thoughts of the diligent tend only to plenteousness; but of every one that is hasty only to want.

Proverbs 21:5

For which of you, intending to build a tower, sitteth not down first, and counteth the cost, whether he have sufficient to finish it?

Luke 14:28

Prepare thy work without, and make it fit for thyself in the field; and afterwards build thine house.

Proverbs 24:27

The ants are a people not strong, yet they prepare their meat in the summer;

Proverbs 30:25

Borrowing and Debt

Agree with thine adversary quickly, whiles thou art in the way with him; lest at any time the adversary deliver thee to the judge, and the judge deliver thee to the officer, and thou be cast into prison.

Matthew 5:25

The stranger that is within thee shall get up above thee very high; and thou shalt come down very low.

He shall lend to thee, and thou shalt not lend to him: he shall be the head, and thou shalt be the tail.

Moreover all these curses shall come upon thee, and shall pursue thee, and overtake thee, till thou be destroyed; because thou hearkenedst not unto the voice of the LORD thy God, to keep his commandments and his statutes which he commanded thee:

Deuteronomy 28:43-45

Withhold not good from them to whom it is due, when it is in the power of thine hand to do it.

Say not unto thy neighbour, Go, and come again, and to morrow I will give; when thou hast it by thee.

Proverbs 3:27-28

The wicked borroweth, and payeth not again: but the righteous sheweth mercy, and giveth.

Psalm 37:21

If he hath wronged thee, or oweth thee ought, put that on mine account;

I Paul have written it with mine own hand, I will repay it: albeit I do not say to thee how thou owest unto me even thine own self besides.

Philemon 1:18-19

The rich ruleth over the poor, and the borrower is servant to the lender.

Proverbs 22:7

Owe no man any thing, but to love one another: for he that loveth another hath fulfilled the law.

Romans 13:8

Lending

For the LORD thy God blesseth thee, as he promised thee: and thou shalt lend unto many nations, but thou shalt not borrow; and thou shalt reign over many nations, but they shall not reign over thee.

Deuteronomy 15:6

And if ye lend to them of whom ye hope to receive, what thank have ye? for sinners also lend to sinners, to receive as much again.

But love ye your enemies, and do good, and lend, hoping for nothing again; and your reward shall be great, and ye shall be the children of the Highest: for he is kind unto the unthankful and to the evil.

Luke 6:34-35

He is ever merciful, and lendeth; and his seed is blessed.

Psalm 37:26

A good man sheweth favour, and lendeth: he will guide his affairs with discretion.

Psalm 112:5

Thou shalt not lend upon usury to thy brother; usury of money, usury of victuals, usury of any thing that is lent upon usury:

Unto a stranger thou mayest lend upon usury; but unto thy brother thou shalt not lend upon usury: that the LORD thy God may bless thee in all that thou settest thine hand to in the land whither thou goest to possess it.

Dueteronomy 23:19-20

If thou lend money to any of my people that is poor by thee, thou shalt not be to him as an usurer, neither shalt thou lay upon him usury.

Exodus 22:25

Tithing

And he looked up, and saw the rich men casting their gifts into the treasury.

And he saw also a certain poor widow casting in thither two mites.

And he said, Of a truth I say unto you, that this poor widow hath cast in more than they all:

For all these have of their abundance cast in unto the offerings of God: but she of her penury hath cast in all the living that she had.

Luke 21:1-4

Even from the days of your fathers ye are gone away from mine ordinances, and have not kept them. Return unto me, and I will return unto you, saith the LORD of hosts. But ye said, Wherein shall we return?

Will a man rob God? Yet ye have robbed me. But ye say, Wherein have we robbed thee? In tithes and offerings.

Ye are cursed with a curse: for ye have robbed me, even this whole nation.

Bring ye all the tithes into the storehouse, that there may be meat in mine house, and prove me now herewith, saith the LORD of hosts, if I will not open you the windows of heaven, and pour you out a blessing, that there shall not be room enough to receive it.

And I will rebuke the devourer for your sakes, and he shall not destroy the fruits of your ground; neither shall your vine cast her fruit before the time in the field, saith the LORD of hosts.

Malachi 3:7-11

And now, behold, I have brought the firstfruits of the land, which thou, O LORD, hast given me. And thou shalt set it before the LORD thy God, and worship before the LORD thy God:

And thou shalt rejoice in every good thing which the LORD thy God hath given unto thee, and unto thine house, thou, and the Levite, and the stranger that is among you.

When thou hast made an end of tithing all the tithes of thine increase the third year, which is the year of tithing, and hast given it unto the Levite, the stranger, the fatherless, and the widow, that they may eat within thy gates, and be filled,

Then thou shalt say before the LORD thy God, I have brought away the hallowed things out of mine house, and also have given them unto the Levite, and unto the stranger, to the fatherless, and to the widow, according to all thy commandments which thou hast commanded me: I have not transgressed thy commandments, neither have I forgotten them:

Deuteronomy 26:10-13

And thither ye shall bring your burnt offerings, and your sacrifices, and your tithes, and heave offerings of your hand, and your vows, and your freewill offerings, and the firstlings of your herds and of your flocks:

Deuteronomy 12:6

And the Levite, (because he hath no part nor inheritance with thee,) and the stranger, and the fatherless, and the widow, which are within thy gates, shall come, and shall eat and be satisfied; that the LORD thy God may bless thee in all the work of thine hand which thou doest.

Deuteronomy 14:29

And God is able to make all grace abound toward you; that ye, always having all sufficiency in all things, may abound to every good work:

(As it is written, He hath dispersed abroad; he hath given to the poor: his righteousness remaineth for ever.

Now he that ministereth seed to the sower both minister bread for your food, and multiply your seed sown, and increase the fruits of your righteousness;)

Being enriched in every thing to all bountifulness, which causeth through us thanksgiving to God.

For the administration of this service not only supplieth the want of the saints, but is abundant also by many thanksgivings unto God;

II Corinthians 9:6-12

And blessed be the most high God, which hath delivered thine enemies into thy hand. And he gave him tithes of all.

Genesis 14:20

For this Melchisedec, king of Salem, priest of the most high God, who met Abraham returning from the slaughter of the kings, and blessed him;

To whom also Abraham gave a tenth part of all; first being by interpretation King of righteousness, and after that also King of Salem, which is, King of peace;

Without father, without mother, without descent, having neither beginning of days, nor end of life; but made like unto the Son of God; abideth a priest continually.

Hebrews 7:1-3

Honour the LORD with thy substance, and with the firstfruits of all thine increase:

So shall thy barns be filled with plenty, and thy presses shall burst out with new wine.

Proverbs 3:9-10

Thou shalt truly tithe all the increase of thy seed, that the field bringeth forth year by year.

And thou shalt eat before the LORD thy God, in the place which he shall choose to place his name there, the tithe of thy corn, of thy wine, and of thine oil, and the firstlings of thy herds and of thy flocks; that thou mayest learn to fear the LORD thy God always.

Deuteronomy 14:22-23

Let him that is taught in the word communicate unto him that teacheth in all good things.

Galatians 6:6

But this I say, He which soweth sparingly shall reap also sparingly; and he which soweth bountifully shall reap also bountifully.

Every man according as he purposeth in his heart, so let him give; not grudgingly, or of necessity: for God loveth a cheerful giver.

II Corinthians 9:6-7

Gifts and Offerings

Every man shall give as he is able, according to the blessing of the LORD thy God which he hath given thee.

Deuteronomy 16:17

And there came a certain poor widow, and she threw in two mites, which make a farthing.

And he called unto him his disciples, and saith unto them, Verily I say unto you, That this poor widow hath cast more in, than all they which have cast into the treasury:

For all they did cast in of their abundance; but she of her want did cast in all that she had, even all her living.

Mark 12:42-44

But this I say, He which soweth sparingly shall reap also sparingly; and he which soweth bountifully shall reap also bountifully.

Every man according as he purposeth in his heart, so let him give; not grudgingly, or of necessity: for God loveth a cheerful giver.

II Corinthians 9:6-7

Honour widows that are widows indeed.

But if any widow have children or nephews, let them learn first to shew piety at home, and to requite their parents: for that is good and acceptable before God.

Now she that is a widow indeed, and desolate, trusteth in God, and continueth in supplications and prayers night and day.

I Timothy 5:3-5

Give, and it shall be given unto you; good measure, pressed down, and shaken together, and running over, shall men give into your bosom. For with the same measure that ye mete withal it shall be measured to you again.

Luke 6:38

Leave there thy gift before the altar, and go thy way; first be reconciled to thy brother, and then come and offer thy gift.

Matthew 5:24

He that hath a bountiful eye shall be blessed; for he giveth of his bread to the poor.

Proverbs 22:9

The liberal soul shall be made fat: and he that watereth shall be watered also himself.

Proverbs 11:25

Helping the Poor

He that despiseth his neighbour sinneth: but he that hath mercy on the poor, happy is he.

Proverbs 14:21

He that oppresseth the poor reproacheth his Maker: but he that honoureth him hath mercy on the poor.

Proverbs 14:31

He that hath pity upon the poor lendeth unto the LORD; and that which he hath given will he pay him again.

Proverbs 19:17

To do justice and judgment is more acceptable to the LORD than sacrifice.

Proverbs 21:3

Sell that ye have, and give alms; provide yourselves bags which wax not old, a treasure in the heavens that faileth not, where no thief approacheth, neither moth corrupteth.

Luke 12:33

He doth execute the judgment of the fatherless and widow, and loveth the stranger, in giving him food and raiment.

Love ye therefore the stranger: for ye were strangers in the land of Egypt.

Deuteronomy 10:18-19

Blessed is he that considereth the poor: the LORD will deliver him in time of trouble.

Psalm 41:1

That they do good, that they be rich in good works, ready to distribute, willing to communicate;

Laying up in store for themselves a good foundation against the time to come, that they may lay hold on eternal life.

I Timothy 6:18-19

Only they would that we should remember the poor; the same which I also was forward to do.

Galatians 2:10

But whoso hath this world's good, and seeth his brother have need, and shutteth up his bowels of compassion from him, how dwelleth the love of God in him?

My little children, let us not love in word, neither in tongue; but in deed and in truth.

I John 3:17-18

What doth it profit, my brethren, though a man say he hath faith, and have not works? can faith save him?

If a brother or sister be naked, and destitute of daily food,

And one of you say unto them, Depart in peace, be ye warmed and filled; notwithstanding ye give them not those things which are needful to the body; what doth it profit?

James 2:14-16

For the poor shall never cease out of the land: therefore I command thee, saying, Thou shalt open thine hand wide unto thy brother, to thy poor, and to thy needy, in thy land.

Deuteronomy 15:11

The righteous considereth the cause of the poor: but the wicked regardeth not to know it.

Proverbs 29:7

He that giveth unto the poor shall not lack: but he that hideth his eyes shall have many a curse.

Proverbs 28:27

For I was an hungred, and ye gave me meat: I was thirsty, and ye gave me drink: I was a stranger, and ye took me in:

Naked, and ye clothed me: I was sick, and ye visited me: I was in prison, and ye came unto me.

And the King shall answer and say unto them, Verily I say unto you,

Inasmuch as ye have done it unto one of the least of these my brethren, ye have done it unto me.

Matthew 25:35-36,40

Surety

A man void of understanding striketh hands, and becometh surety in the presence of his friend.

Proverbs 17:18

Be not thou one of them that strike hands, or of them that are sureties for debts.

If thou hast nothing to pay, why should he take away thy bed from under thee?

Proverbs 22:26-27

He that is surety for a stranger shall smart for it: and he that hateth suretiship is sure.

Proverbs 11:15

Boast not thyself of tomorrow; for thou knowest not what a day may bring forth.

Proverbs 27:1

My son, if thou be surety for thy friend, if thou hast stricken thy hand with a stranger,

Thou art snared with the words of thy mouth, thou art taken with the words of thy mouth.

Do this now, my son, and deliver thyself, when thou art come into the hand of thy friend; go, humble thyself, and make sure thy friend.

Give not sleep to thine eyes, nor slumber to thine eyelids.

Deliver thyself as a roe from the hand of the hunter, and as a bird from the hand of the fowler.

Prov 6:1-5

Take his garment that is surety for a stranger: and take a pledge of him for a strange woman.

Proverbs 20:16

Insurance and Ivestments

There is treasure to be desired and oil in the dwelling of the wise; but a foolish man spendeth it up.

Proverbs 21:20

Go to the ant, thou sluggard; consider her ways, and be wise:

Which having no guide, overseer, or ruler,

Provideth her meat in the summer, and gathereth her food in the harvest.

How long wilt thou sleep, O sluggard? when wilt thou arise out of thy sleep?

Yet a little sleep, a little slumber, a little folding of the hands to sleep:

So shall thy poverty come as one that travelleth, and thy want as an armed man.

Proverbs 6:6-11

The ants are a people not strong, yet they prepare their meat in the summer;

The conies are but a feeble folk, yet make they their houses in the rocks;

Proverbs 30:25-26

Charge them that are rich in this world, that they be not high-minded, nor trust in uncertain riches, but in the living God, who giveth us richly all things to enjoy;

That they do good, that they be rich in good works, ready to distribute, willing to communicate;

Laying up in store for themselves a good foundation against the time to come, that they may lay hold on eternal life.

I Timothy 6:17-19

A prudent man foreseeth the evil, and hideth himself; but the simple pass on, and are punished.

Proverbs 27:12

Labour not to be rich: cease from thine own wisdom.

Wilt thou set thine eyes upon that which is not? for riches certainly make themselves wings; they fly away as an eagle toward heaven.

Be not among winebibbers; among riotous eaters of flesh:

Proverbs 23:4-5,20

For there is a man whose labour is in wisdom, and in knowledge, and in equity; yet to a man that hath not laboured therein shall he leave it for his portion. This also is vanity and a great evil.

Ecclesiastes 2:21

Better is a little with righteousness than great revenues without right.

Proverbs 16:8

If a man beget an hundred children, and live many years, so that the days of his years be many, and his soul be not filled with good, and also that he have no burial; I say, that an untimely birth is better than he.

Ecclesiastes 6:3

Lay not up for yourselves treasures upon earth, where moth and rust doth corrupt, and where thieves break through and steal:

But lay up for yourselves treasures in heaven, where neither moth nor rust doth corrupt, and where thieves do not break through nor steal:

Matthew 6:19-20

And one of the company said unto him, Master, speak to my brother, that he divide the inheritance with me.

And he said unto him, Man, who made me a judge or a divider over you?

And he said unto them, Take heed, and beware of covetousness: for a man's life consisteth not in the abundance of the things which he possesseth.

And he spake a parable unto them, saying, The ground of a certain rich man brought forth plentifully:

And he thought within himself, saying, What shall I do, because I have no room where to bestow my fruits?

And he said, This will I do: I will pull down my barns, and build greater; and there will I bestow all my fruits and my goods.

And I will say to my soul, Soul, thou hast much goods laid up for many years; take thine ease, eat, drink, and be merry.

But God said unto him, Thou fool, this night thy soul shall be required of thee: then whose shall those things be, which thou hast provided?

So is he that layeth up treasure for himself, and is not rich toward God.

Luke 12:13-21

Love not the world, neither the things that are in the world. If any man love the world, the love of the Father is not in him.

For all that is in the world, the lust of the flesh, and the lust of the eyes, and the pride of life, is not of the Father, but is of the world.

I John 2:15-16

Now when Jesus heard these things, he said unto him, Yet lackest thou one thing: sell all that thou hast, and distribute unto the poor, and thou shalt have treasure in heaven: and come, follow me.

Luke 18:22

The thoughts of the diligent tend only to plenteousness; but of every one that is hasty only to want.

Proverbs 21:5

Hoarding

But whoso hath this world's good, and seeth his brother have need, and shutteth up his bowels of compassion from him, how dwelleth the love of God in him?

I John 3:17

So is he that layeth up treasure for himself, and is not rich toward God.

Luke 12:21

Be not thou afraid when one is made rich, when the glory of his house is increased;

For when he dieth he shall carry nothing away: his glory shall not descend after him.

Psalm 49:16-17

Labour not to be rich: cease from thine own wisdom.

Wilt thou set thine eyes upon that which is not? for riches certainly make themselves wings; they fly away as an eagle toward heaven.

Proverbs 23:4-5

For the love of money is the root of all evil: which while some coveted after, they have erred from the faith, and pierced themselves through with many sorrows.

1 Timothy 6:10

He that loveth silver shall not be satisfied with silver; nor he that loveth abundance with increase: this is also vanity.

There is a sore evil which I have seen under the sun, namely, riches kept for the owners thereof to their hurt.

Ecclesiastes 5:10,13

Indulgence

He that loveth pleasure shall be a poor man: he that loveth wine and oil shall not be rich.

Proverbs 21:17

He that trusteth in his own heart is a fool: but whoso walketh wisely, he shall be delivered.

Proverbs 28:26

Let your moderation be known unto all men. The Lord is at hand.

Philippians 4:5

I therefore, the prisoner of the Lord, beseech you that ye walk worthy of the vocation wherewith ye are called,

With all lowliness and meekness, with longsuffering, forbearing one another in love;

Ephesians 4:1-2

Then said Jesus unto his disciples, If any man will come after me, let him deny himself, and take up his cross, and follow me.

Matthew 16:24

The full soul loathes an honeycomb; but the hungry soul every bitter thing is sweet.

Proverbs 27:7

Greed

But fornication, and all uncleanness, or covetousness, let it not be once named among you, as becometh saints;

Ephesians 5:3

From whence come wars and fightings among you? come they not hence, even of your lusts that war in your members?

Ye lust, and have not: ye kill, and desire to have, and cannot obtain: ye fight and war, yet ye have not, because ye ask not.

Know this, that the trying of your faith worket patience.

James 4:1-2

For the wicked boasteth of his heart's desire, and blesseth the covetous, whom the LORD abhorreth.

Psalm 10:3

There is a sore evil which I have seen under the sun, namely, riches kept for the owners thereof to their hurt.

Ecclesiastes 5:13

For from the least of them even unto the greatest of them every one is given to covetousness; and from the prophet even unto the priest every one dealeth falsely.

Jeremiah 6:13

And they come unto thee as the people cometh, and they sit before thee as my people, and they hear thy words, but they will not do them: for with their mouth they shew much love, but their heart goeth after their covetousness.

Ezekiel 33:31

And he said unto them, Take heed, and beware of covetousness: for a man's life consisteth not in the abundance of the things which he possesseth.

So is he that layeth up treasure for himself, and is not rich toward God.

Luke 12:15,21

No servant can serve two masters: for either he will hate the one, and love the other; or else he will hold to the one, and despise the other. Ye cannot serve God and mammon.

And the Pharisees also, who were covetous, heard all these things: and they derided him.

Luke 16:13-14

And many shall follow their pernicious ways; by reason of whom the way of truth shall be evil spoken of.

And through covetousness shall they with feigned words make merchandise of you: whose judgment now of a long time lingereth not, and their damnation slumbereth not.

2 Peter 2:2-3

Suing

Moreover if thy brother shall trespass against thee, go and tell him his fault between thee and him alone: if he shall hear thee, thou hast gained thy brother.

But if he will not hear thee, then take with thee one or two more, that in the mouth of two or three witnesses every word may be established.

And if he shall neglect to hear them, tell it unto the church: but if he neglect to hear the church, let him be unto thee as an heathen man and a publican.

Matthew 18:15-17

Dare any of you, having a matter against another, go to law before the unjust, and not before the saints?

1 Corinthians 6:1

Give to every man that asketh of thee, and of him that taketh away thy goods ask them not again.

And as ye would that men should do to you, do ye also to them likewise.

For if ye love them which love you, what thank have ye? for sinners also love those that love them.

And if ye do good to them which do good to you, what thank have ye? for sinners also do even the same.

And if ye lend to them of whom ye hope to receive, what thank have ye? for sinners also lend to sinners, to receive as much again.

But love ye your enemies, and do good, and lend, hoping for nothing again; and your reward shall be great, and ye shall be the children of the Highest: for he is kind unto the unthankful and to the evil.

Be ye therefore merciful, as your Father also is merciful.

Luke 6:30-36

Obtaining Counsel

He that walketh with wise men shall be wise: but a companion of fools shall be destroyed.

Proverbs 13:20

A wise man will hear, and will increase learning; and a man of understanding shall attain unto wise counsels:

Proverbs 1:5

Go from the presence of a foolish man, when thou perceivest not in him the lips of knowledge.

The simple believeth every word: but the prudent man looketh well to his going.

Proverbs 14:7,15

Give instruction to a wise man, and he will be yet wiser: teach a just man, and he will increase in learning.

Proverbs 9:9

Without counsel purposes are disappointed: but in the multitude of counsellors they are established.

Proverbs 15:22

The way of a fool is right in his own eyes: but he that hearkeneth unto counsel is wise.

Proverbs 12:15

Make no friendship with an angry man; and with a furious man thou shalt not go:

Lest thou learn his ways, and get a snare to thy soul.

Proverbs 22:24-25

Only by pride cometh contention: but with the well advised is wisdom.

Proverbs 13:10

Be not deceived: evil communications corrupt good manners.

1 Corinthians 15:33

Where no counsel is, the people fall: but in the multitude of counsellors there is safety.

Proverbs 11:14

Blessed is the man that walketh not in the counsel of the ungodly, nor standeth in the way of sinners, nor sitteth in the seat of the scornful.

But his delight is in the law of the LORD; and in his law doth he meditate day and night.

And he shall be like a tree planted by the rivers of water, that bringeth forth his fruit in his season; his leaf also shall not wither; and whatsoever he doeth shall prosper.

Psalm 1:1-3

I will bless the LORD, who hath given me counsel: my reins also instruct me in the night seasons.

Psalm 16:7

For by wise counsel thou shalt make thy war: and in multitude of counsellors there is safety.

Proverbs 24:6

Better is a poor and a wise child than an old and foolish king, who will no more be admonished.

Ecclesiastes 4:13

Obedience

No man can serve two masters: for either he will hate the one, and love the other; or else he will hold to the one, and despise the other. Ye cannot serve God and mammon.

Matthew 6:24

He that is faithful in that which is least is faithful also in much: and he that is unjust in the least is unjust also in much.

Luke 16:10

Mine eyes shall be upon the faithful of the land, that they may dwell with me: he that walketh in a perfect way, he shall serve me.

Psalm 101:6

The LORD shall open unto thee his good treasure, the heaven to give the rain unto thy land in his season, and to bless all the work of thine hand: and thou shalt lend unto many nations, and thou shalt not borrow.

And the LORD shall make thee the head, and not the tail; and thou shalt be above only, and thou shalt not be beneath; if that thou hearken unto the commandments of the LORD thy God, which I command thee this day, to observe and to do them:

Deuteronomy 28:12-13

And if it seem evil unto you to serve the LORD, choose you this day whom ye will serve; whether the gods which your fathers served that were on the other side of the flood, or the gods of the Amorites, in whose land ye dwell: but as for me and my house, we will serve the LORD.

Joshua 24:15

Righteousness exalteth a nation: but sin is a reproach to any people.

Proverbs 14:34

Then said Jesus unto his disciples, If any man will come after me, let him deny himself, and take up his cross, and follow me.

Matthew 16:24

But be ye doers of the word, and not hearers only, deceiving your own selves.

James 1:22

What To Do When Finances Cause You To Feel...

Discouraged

Let not your heart be troubled: ye believe in God, believe also in me.

John 14:1

Be careful for nothing; but in every thing by prayer and supplication with thanksgiving let your requests be made known unto God.

And the peace of God, which passeth all understanding, shall keep your hearts and minds through Christ Jesus.

Finally, brethren, whatsoever things are true, whatsoever things are honest, whatsoever things are just, whatsoever things are pure, whatsoever things are lovely, whatsoever things are of good report; if there be any virtue, and if there be any praise, think on these things.

Phiippians 4:6-8

And let us not be weary in well doing: for in due season we shall reap, if we faint not.

Galatians 6:9

Be of good courage, and he shall strengthen your heart, all ye that hope in the LORD.

Psalm 31:24

I know both how to be abased, and I know how to abound: every where and in all things I am instructed both to be full and to be hungry, both to abound and to suffer need.

I can do all things through Christ which strengtheneth me.

Philippians 4:12-13

Ho, every one that thirsteth, come ye to the waters, and he that hath no money; come ye, buy, and eat; yea, come, buy wine and milk without money and without price.

Isaiah 55:1

Blessed are they which do hunger and thirst after righteousness: for they shall be filled.

Matthew 5:6

We are troubled on every side, yet not distressed; we are perplexed, but not in despair;

Persecuted, but not forsaken; cast down, but not destroyed;

2 Corinthians 4:8-9

Peace I leave with you, my peace I give unto you: not as the world giveth, give I unto you. Let not your heart be troubled, neither let it be afraid.

John 14:27

Wait on the LORD: be of good courage, and he shall strengthen thine heart: wait, I say, on the LORD.

Psalm 27:14

Though I walk in the midst of trouble, thou wilt revive me: thou shalt stretch forth thine hand against the wrath of mine enemies, and thy right hand shall save me.

Psalm 138:7 7

Worried

Casting all your care upon him; for he careth for you.

1 Peter 5:7

Thou wilt keep him in perfect peace, whose mind is stayed on thee: because he trusteth in thee.

Isaiah 26:3

And let the peace of God rule in your hearts, to the which also ye are called in one body; and be ye thankful.

Colossians 3:15

Be careful for nothing; but in every thing by prayer and supplication with thanksgiving let your requests be made known unto God.

And the peace of God, which passeth all understanding, shall keep your hearts and minds through Christ Jesus.

Philippians 4:6-7

Therefore I say unto you, Take no thought for your life, what ye shall eat, or what ye shall drink; nor yet for your body, what ye shall put on. Is not the life more than meat, and the body than raiment?

Behold the fowls of the air: for they sow not, neither do they reap, nor gather into barns; yet your heavenly Father feedeth them. Are ye not much better than they?

Which of you by taking thought can add one cubit unto his stature?

And why take ye thought for raiment? Consider the lilies of the field, how they grow; they toil not, neither do they spin:

And yet I say unto you, That even Solomon in all his glory was not arrayed like one of these.

Wherefore, if God so clothe the grass of the field, which to day is, and to morrow is cast into the oven, shall he not much more clothe you, O ye of little faith?

Therefore take no thought, saying, What shall we eat? or, What shall we drink? or, Wherewithal shall we be clothed?

(For after all these things do the Gentiles seek:) for your heavenly Father knoweth that ye have need of all these things.

But seek ye first the kingdom of God, and his righteousness; and all these things shall be added unto you.

Take therefore no thought for the morrow: for the morrow shall take thought for the things of itself. Sufficient unto the day is the evil thereof.

Matthew 6:25-34

When thou liest down, thou shalt not be afraid: yea, thou shalt lie down, and thy sleep shall be sweet.

Proverbs 3:24

Let not your heart be troubled: ye believe in God, believe also in me.

John 14:1

Great peace have they which love thy law: and nothing shall offend them.

Psalm 119:165

Peace I leave with you, my peace I give unto you: not as the world giveth, give I unto you. Let not your heart be troubled, neither let it be afraid.

John 14:27

He that dwelleth in the secret place of the most High shall abide under the shadow of the Almighty.

I will say of the LORD, He is my refuge and my fortress: my God; in him will I trust.

Psalm 91:1-2

The young lions do lack, and suffer hunger: but they that seek the LORD shall not want any good thing.

Psalm 34:10

I know both how to be abased, and I know how to abound: every where and in all things I am instructed both to be full and to be hungry, both to abound and to suffer need.

I can do all things through Christ which strengtheneth me.

Philippians 4:12-13

When the poor and needy seek water, and there is none, and their tongue faileth for thirst, I the LORD will hear them, I the God of Israel will not forsake them.

Isaiah 41:17

Consider the ravens: for they neither sow nor reap; which neither have storehouse nor barn; and God feedeth them: how much more are ye better than the fowls?

And which of you with taking thought can add to his stature one cubit?

If ye then be not able to do that thing which is least, why take ye thought for the rest?

Consider the lilies how they grow: they toil not, they spin not; and yet I say unto you, that Solomon in all his glory was not arrayed like one of these.

If then God so clothe the grass, which is to day in the field, and to morrow is cast into the oven; how much more will he clothe you, O ye of little faith?

Luke 12:24-28

Then shalt thou call, and the LORD shall answer; thou shalt cry, and he shall say, Here I am. If thou take away from the midst of thee the yoke, the putting forth of the finger, and speaking vanity;

And if thou draw out thy soul to the hungry, and satisfy the afflicted soul; then shall thy light rise in obscurity, and thy darkness be as the noonday:

And the LORD shall guide thee continually, and satisfy thy soul in drought, and make fat thy bones: and thou shalt be like a watered garden, and like a spring of water, whose waters fail not.

Isaiah 58:9-11

But I am poor and needy: make haste unto me, O God: thou art my help and my deliverer; O LORD, make no tarrying.

Psalm 70:5

The LORD redeemeth the soul of his servants: and none of them that trust in him shall be desolate.

Psalm 34:22

But my God shall supply all your need according to his riches in glory by Christ Jesus.

Philippians 4:19

I will both lay me down in peace, and sleep: for thou, LORD, only makest me dwell in safety.

Psalm 4:8

I sought the LORD, and he heard me, and delivered me from all my fears.

Psalm 34:4

Trust in the LORD, and do good; so shalt thou dwell in the land, and verily thou shalt be fed.

Psalm 37:3

Angry

He that is slow to wrath is of great understanding: but he that is hasty of spirit exalteth folly.

Proverbs 14:29

He that is slow to anger is better than the mighty; and he that ruleth his spirit than he that taketh a city.

Proverbs 16:32

Let all bitterness, and wrath, and anger, and clamour, and evil speaking, be put away from you, with all malice:

And be ye kind one to another, tenderhearted, forgiving one another, even as God for Christ's sake hath forgiven you.

Ephesians 4:31-32

Be not hasty in thy spirit to be angry: for anger resteth in the bosom of fools.

Ecclesiastes 7:9

Wherefore, my beloved brethren, let every man be swift to hear, slow to speak, slow to wrath:

For the wrath of man worketh not the righteousness of God

James 1:19,20

For if ye forgive men their trespasses, your heavenly Father will also forgive you:

Matthew 6:14

A wise man feareth, and departeth from evil: but the fool rageth, and is confident.

He that is soon angry dealeth foolishly: and a man of wicked devices is hated.

Prov 14:16-17

But now ye also put off all these; anger, wrath, malice, blasphemy, filthy communication out of your mouth.

Colossians 3:8

Cease from anger, and forsake wrath: fret not thyself in any wise to do evil.

Psalm 37:8

Tempted

Wherefore let him that thinketh he standeth take heed lest he fall.

There hath no temptation taken you but such as is common to man: but God is faithful, who will not suffer you to be tempted above that ye are able; but will with the temptation also make a way to escape, that ye may be able to bear it.

1 Corinthians 10:12-13

Wherein ye greatly rejoice, though now for a season, if need be, ye are in heaviness through manifold temptations:

That the trial of your faith, being much more precious than of gold that perisheth, though it be tried with fire, might be found unto praise and honour and glory at the appearing of Jesus Christ:

1 Peter 1:6-7

Blessed is the man that endureth temptation: for when he is tried, he shall receive the crown of life, which the Lord hath promised to them that love him.

James 1:12

Let no man say when he is tempted, I am tempted of God: for God cannot be tempted with evil, neither tempteth he any man:

But every man is tempted, when he is drawn away of his own lust, and enticed.

James 1:13-14

My brethren, count it all joy when ye fall into divers temptations;

Knowing this, that the trying of your faith worketh patience.

James 1:2-3

Submit yourselves therefore to God. Resist the devil, and he will flee from you.

James 4:7

Ye are of God, little children, and have overcome them: because greater is he that is in you, than he that is in the world

I John 4:4.

For we have not an high priest which cannot be touched with the feeling of our infirmities; but was in all points tempted like as we are, yet without sin.

Let us therefore come boldly unto the throne of grace, that we may obtain mercy, and find grace to help in time of need.

Hebrews 4:15-16

The Lord knoweth how to deliver the godly out of temptations, and to reserve the unjust unto the day of judgment to be punished:

2 Peter 2:9

For sin shall not have dominion over you: for ye are not under the law, but under grace.

Romans 6:14

Love not the world, neither the things that are in the world. If any man love the world, the love of the Father is not in him.

For all that is in the world, the lust of the flesh, and the lust of the eyes, and the pride of life, is not of the Father, but is of the world.

I Jn 2:15-16

Thy word have I hid in mine heart, that I might not sin against thee.

Psalm 119:11

Dissatisifed

For he satisfieth the longing soul, and filleth the hungry soul with goodness.

Psalm 107:9

Bless the LORD, O my soul: and all that is within me, bless his holy name.

Bless the LORD, O my soul, and forget not all his benefits:

Who forgiveth all thine iniquities; who healeth all thy diseases;

Who redeemeth thy life from destruction; who crowneth thee with lovingkindness and tender mercies;

Who satisfieth thy mouth with good things; so that thy youth is renewed like the eagle's.

Psalm 103:1-5

A man shall be satisfied with good by the fruit of his mouth: and the recompence of a man's hands shall be rendered unto him.

Proverbs 12:14

And ye shall eat in plenty, and be satisfied, and praise the name of the LORD your God, that hath dealt wondrously with you: and my people shall never be ashamed.

Joel 2:26

Ho, every one that thirsteth, come ye to the waters, and he that hath no money; come ye, buy, and eat; yea, come, buy wine and milk without money and without price.

Isaiah 55:1

O God, thou art my God; early will I seek thee: my soul thirsteth for thee, my flesh longeth for thee in a dry and thirsty land, where no water is;

To see thy power and thy glory, so as I have seen thee in the sanctuary.

Because thy lovingkindness is better than life, my lips shall praise thee.

Thus will I bless thee while I live: I will lift up my hands in thy name.

My soul shall be satisfied as with marrow and fatness; and my mouth shall praise thee with joyful lips:

Psalms 63:1-5

The young lions do lack, and suffer hunger: but they that seek the LORD shall not want any good thing.

Palms 34:10

Better is little with the fear of the LORD than great treasure and trouble therewith.

Proverbs 15:16

Two things have I required of thee; deny me them not before I die:

Remove far from me vanity and lies: give me neither poverty nor riches; feed me with food convenient for me:

Lest I be full, and deny thee, and say, Who is the LORD? or lest I be poor, and steal, and take the name of my God in vain.

Proverbs 30:7-9

The sleep of a labouring man is sweet, whether he eat little or much: but the abundance of the rich will not suffer him to sleep.

Ecclesiastes 5:12

And the soldiers likewise demanded of him, saying, And what shall we do? And he said unto them, Do violence to no man, neither accuse any falsely; and be content with your wages.

Luke 3:14

Blessed are they which do hunger and thirst after righteousness: for they shall be filled.

Matthew 5:6

Not that I speak in respect of want: for I have learned, in whatsoever state I am, therewith to be content.

I know both how to be abased, and I know how to abound: every where and in all things I am instructed both to be full and to be hungry, both to abound and to suffer need.

Philippians 4:11-12

But godliness with contentment is great gain.

For we brought nothing into this world, and it is certain we can carry nothing out.

And having food and raiment let us be therewith content.

1 Timothy 6:6-8

Let your conversation be without covetousness; and be content with such things as ye have: for he hath said, I will never leave thee, nor forsake thee.

Hebrews 13:5

Trust in the LORD, and do good; so shalt thou dwell in the land, and verily thou shalt be fed.

Psalm 37:3

Having confidence in thy obedience I wrote unto thee, knowing that thou wilt also do more than I say.

Philemon 1:21

But godliness with contentment is great gain.

For we brought nothing into this world, and it is certain we can carry nothing out.

And having food and raiment let us be therewith content.

1 Timothy 6:6-8

Confused

Be careful for nothing; but in every thing by prayer and supplication with thanksgiving let your requests be made known unto God.

And the peace of God, which passeth all understanding, shall keep your hearts and minds through Christ Jesus.

Philippians 4:6-7

And thine ears shall hear a word behind thee, saying, This is the way, walk ye in it, when ye turn to the right hand, and when ye turn to the left.

Isaiah 30:21

When thou passest through the waters, I will be with thee; and through the rivers, they shall not overflow thee: when thou walkest through the fire, thou shalt not be burned; neither shall the flame kindle upon thee.

Isaiah 43:2

Cast thy burden upon the LORD, and he shall sustain thee: he shall never suffer the righteous to be moved.

Isaiah 55:22

I will instruct thee and teach thee in the way which thou shalt go: I will guide thee with mine eye.

Psalm 32:8

If any of you lack wisdom, let him ask of God, that giveth to all men liberally, and upbraideth not; and it shall be given him.

James 1:5

For the Lord GOD will help me; therefore shall I not be confounded: therefore have I set my face like a flint, and I know that I shall not be ashamed.

Isaiah 50:7 7

For where envying and strife is, there is confusion and every evil work.

But the wisdom that is from above is first pure, then peaceable, gentle, and easy to be intreated, full of mercy and good fruits, without partiality, and without hypocrisy.

And the fruit of righteousness is sown in peace of them that make peace.

James 3:16-18

For God hath not given us the spirit of fear; but of power, and of love, and of a sound mind.

2 Timothy 1:7

For God is not the author of confusion, but of peace, as in all churches of the saints.

1 Corinthians 14:33

Great peace have they which love thy law: and nothing shall offend them.

Psalm 119:165

What To Do When...

You Face Financial Trouble

Be careful for nothing; but in every thing by prayer and supplication with thanksgiving let your requests be made known unto God.

And the peace of God, which passeth all understanding, shall keep your hearts and minds through Christ Jesus.

Philippians 4:6-7

Blessed be God, even the Father of our Lord Jesus Christ, the Father of mercies, and the God of all comfort;

Who comforteth us in all our tribulation, that we may be able to comfort them which are in any trouble, by the comfort wherewith we ourselves are comforted of God.

2 Corinthians 1:3-4

Casting all your care upon him; for he careth for you.

1 Peter 5:7

For we have not an high priest which cannot be touched with the feeling of our infirmities; but was in all points tempted like as we are, yet without sin.

Let us therefore come boldly unto the throne of grace, that we may obtain mercy, and find grace to help in time of need.

Hebrews 4:15-16

I will lift up mine eyes unto the hills, from whence cometh my help.

My help cometh from the LORD, which made heaven and earth.

Psalm 121:1-2

I will be glad and rejoice in thy mercy: for thou hast considered my trouble; thou hast known my soul in adversities;

Psalm 31:7

When thou passest through the waters, I will be with thee; and through the rivers, they shall not overflow thee: when thou walkest through the fire, thou shalt not be burned; neither shall the flame kindle upon thee.

Isaiah 43:2

Let not your heart be troubled: ye believe in God, believe also in me.

John 14:1

Many are the afflictions of the righteous: but the LORD delivereth him out of them all.

Psalm 34:19

Though I walk in the midst of trouble, thou wilt revive me: thou shalt stretch forth thine hand against the wrath of mine enemies, and thy right hand shall save me.

Psalm 138:7

We are troubled on every side, yet not distressed; we are perplexed, but not in despair;

Persecuted, but not forsaken; cast down, but not destroyed;

2 Corinthians 4:8-9

The LORD is good, a strong hold in the day of trouble; and he knoweth them that trust in him.

Nahum 1:7

Come unto me, all ye that labour and are heavy laden, and I will give you rest.

Take my yoke upon you, and learn of me; for I am meek and lowly in heart: and ye shall find rest unto your souls.

Matthew 11:28-29

Peace I leave with you, my peace I give unto you: not as the world giveth, give I unto you. Let not your heart be troubled, neither let it be afraid.

John 14:27

Likewise the Spirit also helpeth our infirmities: for we know not what we should pray for as we ought: but the Spirit itself maketh intercession for us with groanings which cannot be uttered.

And we know that all things work together for good to them that love God, to them who are the called according to his purpose.

What shall we then say to these things? If God be for us, who can be against us?

Romans 8:26,28,31

You Don't Understand God's Plan

The LORD will perfect that which concerneth me: thy mercy, O LORD, endureth for ever: forsake not the works of thine own hands.

Psalm 138:8

Let us hold fast the profession of our faith without wavering; (for he is faithful that promised;)

Hebrews 10:23

As for God, his way is perfect: the word of the LORD is tried: he is a buckler to all those that trust in him.

Psalm 18:30

Cast thy burden upon the LORD, and he shall sustain thee: he shall never suffer the righteous to be moved.

Psalm 55:22

For I know the thoughts that I think toward you, saith the LORD, thoughts of peace, and not of evil, to give you an expected end.

Then shall ye call upon me, and ye shall go and pray unto me, and I will hearken unto you.

And ye shall seek me, and find me, when ye shall search for me with all your heart.

And I will be found of you, saith the LORD: and I will turn away your captivity, and I will gather you from all the nations, and from all the places whither I have driven you, saith the LORD; and I will bring you again into the place whence I caused you to be carried away captive.

Jeremiah 29:11-14

Then shall we know, if we follow on to know the LORD: his going forth is prepared as the morning; and he shall come unto us as the rain, as the latter and former rain unto the earth.

Hosea 6:3

Fear thou not; for I am with thee: be not dismayed; for I am thy God: I will strengthen thee; yea, I will help thee; yea, I will uphold thee with the right hand of my righteousness.

Isaiah 41:10

For my thoughts are not your thoughts, neither are your ways my ways, saith the LORD.

For as the heavens are higher than the earth, so are my ways higher than your ways, and my thoughts than your thoughts.

Isaiah 55:8-9

For the Lord GOD will help me; therefore shall I not be confounded: therefore have I set my face like a flint, and I know that I shall not be ashamed.

Isaiah 50:7

If any of you lack wisdom, let him ask of God, that giveth to all men liberally, and upbraideth not; and it shall be given him.

James 1:5

Trust in the LORD with all thine heart; and lean not unto thine own understanding.

In all thy ways acknowledge him, and he shall direct thy paths.

Proverbs 3:5-6

Great peace have they which love thy law: and nothing shall offend them.

Psalm 119:165

Be careful for nothing; but in every thing by prayer and supplication with thanksgiving let your requests be made known unto God.

And the peace of God, which passeth all understanding, shall keep your hearts and minds through Christ Jesus.

Philippians 4:6-7

Many sorrows shall be to the wicked: but he that trusteth in the LORD, mercy shall compass him about.

Psalm 32:10

And we know that all things work together for good to them that love God, to them who are the called according to his purpose.

Romans 8:28

Waiting On God For An Answer

Let us hold fast the profession of our faith without wavering; (for he is faithful that promised;)

Hebrews 10:23

But they that wait upon the LORD shall renew their strength; they shall mount up with wings as eagles; they shall run, and not be weary; and they shall walk, and not faint.

Isaiah 40:31

For the vision is yet for an appointed time, but at the end it shall speak, and not lie: though it tarry, wait for it; because it will surely come, it will not tarry.

Habakkuk 2:3

My soul, wait thou only upon God; for my expectation is from him.

Psalm 62:5

Wait on the LORD: be of good courage, and he shall strengthen thine heart: wait, I say, on the LORD.

Psalm 27:14

And it shall be said in that day, Lo, this is our God; we have waited for him, and he will save us: this is the LORD; we have waited for him, we will be glad and rejoice in his salvation.

Isaiah 25:9

The eyes of all wait upon thee; and thou givest them their meat in due season.

Thou openest thine hand, and satisfiest the desire of every living thing.

Psalm 145:15-16

You Are Dissatisfied About Work

Behold, God is my salvation; I will trust, and not be afraid: for the LORD JEHOVAH is my strength and my song; he also is become my salvation.

Therefore with joy shall ye draw water out of the wells of salvation.

Isaiah 12:2-3

And God is able to make all grace abound toward you; that ye, always having all sufficiency in all things, may abound to every good work:

2 Corinthians 9:8

A man shall be satisfied with good by the fruit of his mouth: and the recompence of a man's hands shall be rendered unto him.

Proverbs 12:14

Trust in the LORD, and do good; so shalt thou dwell in the land, and verily thou shalt be fed.

Psalm 37:3

O God, thou art my God; early will I seek thee: my soul thirsteth for thee, my flesh longeth for thee in a dry and thirsty land, where no water is;

To see thy power and thy glory, so as I have seen thee in the sanctuary.

Because thy lovingkindness is better than life, my lips shall praise thee.

Thus will I bless thee while I live: I will lift up my hands in thy name.

My soul shall be satisfied as with marrow and fatness; and my mouth shall praise thee with joyful lips:

Psalm 63:1-5

In every thing give thanks: for this is the will of God in Christ Jesus concerning you.

1Thessalonians 5:18

He that is faithful in that which is least is faithful also in much: and he that is unjust in the least is unjust also in much.

Luke 16:10

Two things have I required of thee; deny me them not before I die:

Remove far from me vanity and lies: give me neither poverty nor riches; feed me with food convenient for me:

Lest I be full, and deny thee, and say, Who is the LORD? or lest I be poor, and steal, and take the name of my God in vain.

Proverbs 30:7-9

The sleep of a labouring man is sweet, whether he eat little or much: but the abundance of the rich will not suffer him to sleep.

Ecclesiastes 5:12

Let your conversation be without covetousness; and be content with such things as ye have: for he hath said, I will never leave thee, nor forsake thee.

Hebrews 13:5

Let your light so shine before men, that they may see your good works, and glorify your Father which is in heaven.

Matthew 5:16

And whatsoever ye do, do it heartily, as to the Lord, and not unto men;

Colossians 3:23

Let him that stole steal no more: but rather let him labour, working with his hands the thing which is good, that he may have to give to him that needeth.

Ephesians 4:28

Therefore he brought down their heart with labour; they fell down, and there was none to help.

Then they cried unto the LORD in their trouble, and he saved them out of their distresses.

Psalm 107:12-13

In the sweat of thy face shalt thou eat bread, till thou return unto the ground; for out of it wast thou taken: for dust thou art, and unto dust shalt thou return.

Genesis 3:19

For even when we were with you, this we commanded you, that if any would not work, neither should he eat.

II Thessalonians 3:10

And the soldiers likewise demanded of him, saying, And what shall we do? And he said unto them, Do violence to no man, neither accuse any falsely; and be content with your wages.

Luke 3:14

Not that I speak in respect of want: for I have learned, in whatsoever state I am, therewith to be content.

Philippians 4:11

And having food and raiment let us be therewith content.

1 Timothy 6:8

And that ye study to be quiet, and to do your own business, and to work with your own hands, as we commanded you;

That ye may walk honestly toward them that are without, and that ye may have lack of nothing.

1Thessalonians 4:11-12

The husbandman that laboureth must be first partaker of the fruits.

2 Timothy 2:6

God's Plan of Action For...

Sales & Service

Let your speech be alway with grace, seasoned with salt, that ye may know how ye ought to answer every man.

Colossians 4:6

And whatsoever ye do, do it heartily, as to the Lord, and not unto men;

Colossians 3:23

Ye are the light of the world. A city that is set on an hill cannot be hid.

Neither do men light a candle, and put it under a bushel, but on a candlestick; and it giveth light unto all that are in the house.

Let your light so shine before men, that they may see your good works, and glorify your Father which is in heaven.

Matthew 5:14-16

And he sat down, and called the twelve, and saith unto them, If any man desire to be first, the same shall be last of all, and servant of all.

Mark 9:35

Be not deceived; God is not mocked: for whatsoever a man soweth, that shall he also reap.

For he that soweth to his flesh shall of the flesh reap corruption; but he that soweth to the Spirit shall of the Spirit reap life everlasting.

And let us not be weary in well doing: for in due season we shall reap, if we faint not.

As we have therefore opportunity, let us do good unto all men, especially unto them who are of the household of faith.

Galatians 6:7-10

Whatsoever thy hand findeth to do, do it with thy might; for there is no work, nor device, nor knowledge, nor wisdom, in the grave, whither thou goest.

Ecclesiastes 9:10

For, brethren, ye have been called unto liberty; only use not liberty for an occasion to the flesh, but by love serve one another.

For all the law is fulfilled in one word, even in this; Thou shalt love thy neighbour as thyself.

Galatians 5:13-14

Then said Jesus unto his disciples, If any man will come after me, let him deny himself, and take up his cross, and follow me.

For whosoever will save his life shall lose it: and whosoever will lose his life for my sake shall find it.

For what is a man profited, if he shall gain the whole world, and lose his own soul? or what shall a man give in exchange for his soul?

Matthew 16:24-26

So after he had washed their feet, and had taken his garments, and was set down again, he said unto them, Know ye what I have done to you?

Ye call me Master and Lord: and ye say well; for so I am.

If I then, your Lord and Master, have washed your feet; ye also ought to wash one another's feet.

For I have given you an example, that ye should do as I have done to you.

John 13:12-15

But made himself of no reputation, and took upon him the form of a servant, and was made in the likeness of men:

And being found in fashion as a man, he humbled himself, and became obedient unto death, even the death of the cross.

Phliippians 2:7-8

No servant can serve two masters: for either he will hate the one, and love the other; or else he will hold to the one, and despise the other. Ye cannot serve God and mammon.

Luke 16:13

But it shall not be so among you: but whosoever will be great among you, let him be your minister;

And whosoever will be chief among you, let him be your servant:

Matthew 20:26-27

Now it came to pass, as they went, that he entered into a certain village: and a certain woman named Martha received him into her house.

And she had a sister called Mary, which also sat at Jesus' feet, and heard his word.

But Martha was cumbered about much serving, and came to him, and said, Lord, dost thou not care that my sister hath left me to serve alone? bid her therefore that she help me.

And Jesus answered and said unto her, Martha, Martha, thou art careful and troubled about many things:

But one thing is needful: and Mary hath chosen that good part, which shall not be taken away from her.

Luke 10:38-42

Work and Wages

Commit thy works unto the LORD, and thy thoughts shall be established.

Proverbs 16:3

For even when we were with you, this we commanded you, that if any would not work, neither should he eat.

II Thessalonians 3:10

Servants, be obedient to them that are your masters according to the flesh, with fear and trembling, in singleness of your heart, as unto Christ;

Not with eyeservice, as men-pleasers; but as the servants of Christ, doing the will of God from the heart;

With good will doing service, as to the Lord, and not to men:

Ephesians 6:5-7

And whatsoever ye do, do it heartily, as to the Lord, and not unto men;

Colossians 3:23

Behold that which I have seen: it is good and comely for one to eat and to drink, and to enjoy the good of all his labour that he taketh under the sun all the days of his life, which God giveth him: for it is his portion.

Every man also to whom God hath given riches and wealth, and hath given him power to eat thereof, and to take his portion, and to rejoice in his labour; this is the gift of God.

Ecclesiastes 5:18-19

Let him that stole steal no more: but rather let him labour, working with his hands the thing which is good, that he may have to give to him that needeth.

Ephesians 4:28

That ye may walk honestly toward them that are without, and that ye may have lack of nothing.

1Thessalonians 4:12

The labour of the righteous tendeth to life: the fruit of the wicked to sin.

Proverbs 10:16

Woe unto him that buildeth his house by unrighteousness, and his chambers by wrong; that useth his neighbour's service without wages, and giveth him not for his work;

Jeremiah 22:13

Even so hath the Lord ordained that they which preach the gospel should live of the gospel.

1 Corinthians 9:14

And I will come near to you to judgment; and I will be a swift witness against the sorcerers, and against the adulterers, and against false swearers, and against those that oppress the hireling in his wages, the widow, and the fatherless, and that turn aside the stranger from his right, and fear not me, saith the LORD of hosts.

Malachi 3:5

Provide neither gold, nor silver, nor brass in your purses,

Nor scrip for your journey, neither two coats, neither shoes, nor yet staves: for the workman is worthy of his meat.

Matthew 10:9-10

It is vain for you to rise up early, to sit up late, to eat the bread of sorrows: for so he giveth his beloved sleep.

Psalm 127:2

And the soldiers likewise demanded of him, saying, And what shall we do? And he said unto them, Do violence to no man, neither accuse any falsely; and be content with your wages.

Luke 3:14

For the scripture saith, Thou shalt not muzzle the ox that treadeth out the corn. And, The labourer is worthy of his reward.

1 Timohy 5:18

Which have borne witness of thy charity before the church: whom if thou bring forward on their journey after a godly sort, thou shalt do well:

Because that for his name's sake they went forth, taking nothing of the Gentiles.

3 John 6-7

No man that warreth entangleth himself with the affairs of this life; that he may please him who hath chosen him to be a soldier.

The husbandman that laboureth must be first partaker of the fruits.

2 Timothy 2:4,6

And the LORD God took the man, and put him into the garden of Eden to dress it and to keep it.

Genesis 2:15

Let your light so shine before men, that they may see your good works, and glorify your Father which is in heaven.

Matthew 5:16

And in the same house remain, eating and drinking such things as they give: for the labourer is worthy of his hire. Go not from house to house.

Luke 10:7

Planning & Goal Setting

Trust in the LORD with all thine heart; and lean not unto thine own understanding.

In all thy ways acknowledge him, and he shall direct thy paths.

Proverbs 3:5-6

Hear counsel, and receive instruction, that thou mayest be wise in thy latter end.

There are many devices in a man's heart; nevertheless the counsel of the LORD, that shall stand.

Proverbs 19:20-21

I will instruct thee and teach thee in the way which thou shalt go: I will guide thee with mine eye.

Psalm 32:8

Shew me thy ways, O LORD; teach me thy paths.

Psalm 25:4

A man's heart deviseth his way: but the LORD directeth his steps.

Proverbs 16:9

For which of you, intending to build a tower, sitteth not down first, and counteth the cost, whether he have sufficient to finish it?

Lest haply, after he hath laid the foundation, and is not able to finish it, all that behold it begin to mock him,

Saying, This man began to build, and was not able to finish.

Or what king, going to make war against another king, sitteth not down first, and consulteth whether he be able with ten thousand to meet him that cometh against him with twenty thousand?

Or else, while the other is yet a great way off, he sendeth an ambassage, and desireth conditions of peace.

Luke 14:28-32

Without counsel purposes are disappointed: but in the multitude of counsellors they are established.

Proverbs 15:22

Counsel in the heart of man is like deep water; but a man of understanding will draw it out.

Proverbs 20:5

For by wise counsel thou shalt make thy war: and in multitude of counsellors there is safety.

Proverbs 24:6

The steps of a good man are ordered by the LORD: and he delighteth in his way.

Psalm 37:23

Go not forth hastily to strive, lest thou know not what to do in the end thereof, when thy neighbour hath put thee to shame.

Proverbs 25:8

The simple believeth every word: but the prudent man looketh well to his going.

Proverbs 14:15

Prepare thy work without, and make it fit for thyself in the field; and afterwards build thine house.

Proverbs 24:27

A prudent man foreseeth the evil, and hideth himself; but the simple pass on, and are punished.

Proverbs 27:12

Be thou diligent to know the state of thy flocks, and look well to thy herds.

For riches are not for ever: and doth the crown endure to every generation?

Proverbs 27:23-24

The ants are a people not strong, yet they prepare their meat in the summer;

Proverbs 30:25

Times of Crisis

I will lift up mine eyes unto the hills, from whence cometh my help.

My help cometh from the LORD, which made heaven and earth.

Psalm 121:1-2

But my God shall supply all your need according to his riches in glory by Christ Jesus.

Philippians 4:19

Casting all your care upon him; for he careth for you.

1 Peter 5:7

If my people, which are called by my name, shall humble themselves, and pray, and seek my face, and turn from their wicked ways; then will I hear from heaven, and will forgive their sin, and will heal their land.

2 Chronicles 7:14

Why art thou cast down, O my soul? and why art thou disquieted within me? hope in God: for I shall yet praise him, who is the health of my countenance, and my God.

Psalm 43:5

Be strong and of a good courage, fear not, nor be afraid of them: for the LORD thy God, he it is that doth go with thee; he will not fail thee, nor forsake thee.

Deuteronomy 31:6

Because he hath set his love upon me, therefore will I deliver him: I will set him on high, because he hath known my name.

He shall call upon me, and I will answer him: I will be with him in trouble; I will deliver him, and honour him.

Psalm 91:14-15

The LORD is good, a strong hold in the day of trouble; and he knoweth them that trust in him.

Nahum 1:7

Beloved, think it not strange concerning the fiery trial which is to try you, as though some strange thing happened unto you:

But rejoice, inasmuch as ye are partakers of Christ's sufferings; that, when his glory shall be revealed, ye may be glad also with exceeding joy.

1 Peter 4:12-13

Blessed be God, even the Father of our Lord Jesus Christ, the Father of mercies, and the God of all comfort;

Who comforteth us in all our tribulation, that we may be able to comfort them which are in any trouble, by the comfort wherewith we ourselves are comforted of God.

2 Corinthians 1:3-4

We are troubled on every side, yet not distressed; we are perplexed, but not in despair;

Persecuted, but not forsaken; cast down, but not destroyed;

2 Corinthians 4:8-9

Therefore take no thought, saying, What shall we eat? or, What shall we drink? or, Wherewithal shall we be clothed?

(For after all these things do the Gentiles seek:) for your heavenly Father knoweth that ye have need of all these things.

But seek ye first the kingdom of God, and his righteousness; and all these things shall be added unto you.

Matthew 6:31-33

Though I walk in the midst of trouble, thou wilt revive me: thou shalt stretch forth thine hand against the wrath of mine enemies, and thy right hand shall save me.

Psalm 138:7

And we know that all things work together for good to them that love God, to them who are the called according to his purpose.

Romans 8:28

Dealing With Business Failure

It is better to trust in the LORD than to put confidence in man.

Psalm 118:8

Therefore, brethren, stand fast, and hold the traditions which ye have been taught, whether by word, or our epistle.

Now our Lord Jesus Christ himself, and God, even our Father, which hath loved us, and hath given us everlasting consolation and good hope through grace,

Comfort your hearts, and stablish you in every good word and work.

II Thessalonians 2:15-17

It is vain for you to rise up early, to sit up late, to eat the bread of sorrows: for so he giveth his beloved sleep.

Psalm 127:2

Ye ask, and receive not, because ye ask amiss, that ye may consume it upon your lusts.

James 4:3

Strengthen ye the weak hands, and confirm the feeble knees.

Say to them that are of a fearful heart, Be strong, fear not: behold, your God will come with vengeance, even God with a recompence; he will come and save you.

Then the eyes of the blind shall be opened, and the ears of the deaf shall be unstopped.

Then shall the lame man leap as an hart, and the tongue of the dumb sing: for in the wilderness shall waters break out, and streams in the desert.

Isaiah 35:3-6

For I am persuaded, that neither death, nor life, nor angels, nor principalities, nor powers, nor things present, nor things to come,

Nor height, nor depth, nor any other creature, shall be able to separate us from the love of God, which is in Christ Jesus our Lord.

Romans 8:38-39

And we know that all things work together for good to them that love God, to them who are the called according to his purpose.

Romans 8:28

Pride goeth before destruction, and an haughty spirit before a fall.

Proverbs 16:18

But he that is greatest among you shall be your servant.

And whosoever shall exalt himself shall be abased; and he that shall humble himself shall be exalted.

Matthew 23:11-12

But Jesus called them unto him, and said, Ye know that the princes of the Gentiles exercise dominion over them, and they that are great exercise authority upon them.

But it shall not be so among you: but whosoever will be great among you, let him be your minister;

And whosoever will be chief among you, let him be your servant:

Matthew 20:25-27

Let nothing be done through strife or vainglory; but in lowliness of mind let each esteem other better than themselves.

Philippians 2:3

For whosoever exalteth himself shall be abased; and he that humbleth himself shall be exalted.

Luke 14:11

Better is the poor that walketh in his integrity, than he that is perverse in his lips, and is a fool.

Proverbs 19:1

Now unto him that is able to do exceeding abundantly above all that we ask or think, according to the power that worketh in us,

Unto him be glory in the church by Christ Jesus throughout all ages, world without end. Amen.

Ephesians 3:20,21

Handling Financial Surplus

He that is faithful in that which is least is faithful also in much: and he that is unjust in the least is unjust also in much.

If therefore ye have not been faithful in the unrighteous mammon, who will commit to your trust the true riches?

Luke 16:10-11

A good name is rather to be chosen than great riches, and loving favour rather than silver and gold.

Proverbs 22:1

By humility and the fear of the LORD are riches, and honour, and life.

Proverbs 22:4

A man's pride shall bring him low: but honour shall uphold the humble in spirit.

Proverbs 29:23

Let nothing be done through strife or vainglory; but in lowliness of mind let each esteem other better than themselves.

Philippians 2:3

No man can serve two masters: for either he will hate the one, and love the other; or else he will hold to the one, and despise the other. Ye cannot serve God and mammon.

Matthew 6:24

Take heed therefore how ye hear: for whosoever hath, to him shall be given; and whosoever hath not, from him shall be taken even that which he seemeth to have.

Luke 8:18

Then Peter and the other apostles answered and said, We ought to obey God rather than men.

Acts 5:29

But God said unto him, Thou fool, this night thy soul shall be required of thee: then whose shall those things be, which thou hast provided?

So is he that layeth up treasure for himself, and is not rich toward God.

For where your treasure is, there will your heart be also.

Luke 12:20-21, 34

Whoso stoppeth his ears at the cry of the poor, he also shall cry himself, but shall not be heard.

Proverbs 21:13

He that walketh uprightly walketh surely: but he that perverteth his ways shall be known.

Proverbs 10:9

I the LORD search the heart, I try the reins, even to give every man according to his ways, and according to the fruit of his doings.

As the partridge sitteth on eggs, and hatcheth them not; so he that getteth riches, and not by right, shall leave them in the midst of his days, and at his end shall be a fool.

Jeremiah 17:10-11

Charge them that are rich in this world, that they be not highminded, nor trust in uncertain riches, but in the living God, who giveth us richly all things to enjoy;

That they do good, that they be rich in good works, ready to distribute, willing to communicate;

1 Timothy 6:17-18

Behold that which I have seen: it is good and comely for one to eat and to drink, and to enjoy the good of all his labour that he taketh under the sun all the days of his life, which God giveth him: for it is his portion.

Every man also to whom God hath given riches and wealth, and hath given him power to eat thereof, and to take his portion, and to rejoice in his labour; this is the gift of God.

For he shall not much remember the days of his life; because God answereth him in the joy of his heart.

Ecclesiastes 5:18-20

Growing Older

Trust in the LORD with all thine heart; and lean not unto thine own understanding.

In all thy ways acknowledge him, and he shall direct thy paths.

Be not wise in thine own eyes: fear the LORD, and depart from evil.

It shall be health to thy navel, and marrow to thy bones.

Honour the LORD with thy substance, and with the firstfruits of all thine increase:

So shall thy barns be filled with plenty, and thy presses shall burst out with new wine.

Proverbs 3:5-10

Rest in the LORD, and wait patiently for him: fret not thyself because of him who prospereth in his way, because of the man who bringeth wicked devices to pass.

Psalm 37:7

Happy is the man that findeth wisdom, and the man that getteth understanding.

For the merchandise of it is better than the merchandise of silver, and the gain thereof than fine gold.

She is more precious than rubies: and all the things thou canst desire are not to be compared unto her.

Length of days is in her right hand; and in her left hand riches and honour.

Proverbs 3:13-16

Beloved, I wish above all things that thou mayest prosper and be in health, even as thy soul prospereth.

For I rejoiced greatly, when the brethren came and testified of the truth that is in thee, even as thou walkest in the truth.

3 John 2-3

This book of the law shall not depart out of thy mouth; but thou shalt meditate therein day and night, that thou mayest observe to do according to all that is written therein: for then thou shalt make thy way prosperous, and then thou shalt have good success.

Joshua 1:8

A little that a righteous man hath is better than the riches of many wicked.

For the arms of the wicked shall be broken: but the LORD upholdeth the righteous.

The LORD knoweth the days of the upright: and their inheritance shall be for ever.

They shall not be ashamed in the evil time: and in the days of famine they shall be satisfied.

Psalm 37:16-19

But God forbid that I should glory, save in the cross of our Lord Jesus Christ, by whom the world is crucified unto me, and I unto the world.

Galatians 6:14

Hear, O LORD, and have mercy upon me: LORD, be thou my helper.

Thou hast turned for me my mourning into dancing: thou hast put off my sackcloth, and girded me with gladness;

To the end that my glory may sing praise to thee, and not be silent. O LORD my God, I will give thanks unto thee for ever.

Psalm 30:10-12

Two things have I required of thee; deny me them not before I die:

Remove far from me vanity and lies: give me neither poverty nor riches; feed me with food convenient for me:

Lest I be full, and deny thee, and say, Who is the LORD? or lest I be poor, and steal, and take the name of my God in vain.

Proverbs 30:7-9

Lay not up for yourselves treasures upon earth, where moth and rust doth corrupt, and where thieves break through and steal:

But lay up for yourselves treasures in heaven, where neither moth nor rust doth corrupt, and where thieves do not break through nor steal:

Matthew 6:19-20

The sleep of a labouring man is sweet, whether he eat little or much: but the abundance of the rich will not suffer him to sleep.

There is a sore evil which I have seen under the sun, namely, riches kept for the owners thereof to their hurt.

But those riches perish by evil travail: and he begetteth a son, and there is nothing in his hand.

As he came forth of his mother's womb, naked shall he return to go as he came, and shall take nothing of his labour, which he may carry away in his hand.

And this also is a sore evil, that in all points as he came, so shall he go: and what profit hath he that hath laboured for the wind?

Ecclesiastes 5:12-16

Blessed is he whose transgression is forgiven, whose sin is covered.

Psalm 32:1

Behold that which I have seen: it is good and comely for one to eat and to drink, and to enjoy the good of all his labour that he taketh under the sun all the days of his life, which God giveth him: for it is his portion.

Every man also to whom God hath given riches and wealth, and hath given him power to eat thereof, and to take his portion, and to rejoice in his labour; this is the gift of God.

For he shall not much remember the days of his life; because God answereth him in the joy of his heart.

Ecclesiastes 5:18-20

God's Plan For Eternal Life

Eternal Life

For all have sinned, and come short of the glory of God;

Romans 3:23

For the wages of sin is death; but the gift of God is eternal life through Jesus Christ our Lord.

Romans 6:23

But God commendeth his love toward us, in that, while we were yet sinners, Christ died for us.

Romans 5:8

But what saith it? The word is nigh thee, even in thy mouth, and in thy heart: that is, the word of faith, which we preach;

That if thou shalt confess with thy mouth the Lord Jesus, and shalt believe in thine heart that God hath raised him from the dead, thou shalt be saved.

For with the heart man believeth unto righteousness; and with the mouth confession is made unto salvation.

Romans 10:8-10

For whosoever shall call upon the name of the Lord shall be saved.

Romans 10:13

Wherefore, as by one man sin entered into the world, and death by sin; and so death passed upon all men, for that all have sinned:

Romans 5:12

For God so loved the world, that he gave his only begotten Son, that whosoever believeth in him should not perish, but have everlasting life.

For God sent not his Son into the world to condemn the world; but that the world through him might be saved.

John 3:16-17

He that believeth on the Son hath everlasting life: and he that believeth not the Son shall not see life; but the wrath of God abideth on him.

John 3:36

But as many as received him, to them gave he power to become the sons of God, even to them that believe on his name:

John 1:12

For by grace are ye saved through faith; and that not of yourselves: it is the gift of God:

Not of works, lest any man should boast.

Ephesians 2:8-9

Whosoever therefore shall confess me before men, him will I confess also before my Father which is in heaven.

Matthew 10:32

Verily, verily, I say unto you, He that believeth on me hath everlasting life.

John 6:47

And this is the record, that God hath given to us eternal life, and this life is in His Son.

He that hath the Son hath life; and he that hath not the Son of God hath not life.

These things I have written unto you that believe on the name of the Son of God; that ye may know that ye have eternal life, and that ye may believe on the name of the Son of God.

1 John 5:11-13

That if thou shalt confess with thy mouth the Lord Jesus, and shalt believe in thine heart that God hath raised him from the dead, thou shalt be saved.

Romans 10:9

Verily, verily, I say unto you, He that heareth my word, and believeth on him that sent me, hath everlasting life, and shall not come into condemnation; but is passed from death unto life.

John 5:24

PERSONAL STUDY NOTES

PERSONAL STUDY NOTES

PERSONAL STUDY NOTES

PERSONAL STUDY NOTES

PERSONAL STUDY NOTES

PERSONAL STUDY NOTES

PERSONAL STUDY NOTES

PERSONAL STUDY NOTES

PERSONAL STUDY NOTES

PERSONAL STUDY NOTES

PERSONAL STUDY NOTES

PERSONAL STUDY NOTES

PERSONAL STUDY NOTES

MY PRAYER LIST

MY PRAYER LIST